Why Me?
Why Not?

*Making the Most
Out of What You Have*

By
Tim Goonan

Little Giants Publishing, Inc.

Why Me? Why Not?
Making the Most Out of What You Have
By Tim Goonan

Copyright 2005
Little Giants Publishing , Inc.
Hendersonville, Tennessee 37075

Library of Congress Control Number: 2005927824
ISBN 0-9770021-0-1

Cover design by Rick Milewski
Concept by Lilian Brooks
Photos by Samantha Goonan

All dictionary quotations by permission from
Merriam-Webster's Collegiate® Dictionary, Eleventh
Edition ©2004 by Merriam-Webster, Incorporated
(Merriam-Webster.com).

Printed in the United States.

I would like to thank Bob Dean for his encouragement on the back row at church to write this book. I wouldn't have told my story to anyone without him.
I would also like to thank Jeff Flint and Mike McClanahan for their help and friendship.
I dedicate this book to my children T.J, Samantha, Mariah, and Caleb. Dad loves you! The last dedication and thanks goes to My Father in Heaven and His Son Jesus for making my life complete.

Contents

Foreword

I first met Tim Goonan at a church we were both attending. I didn't notice the cane until I saw him with it several times. My first thought was that he may be a little eccentric, until I found out the rest of the story. Tim's life and friendship have opened my eyes to many other things, along with giving me a heart to notice people's struggles. I, like most folks, have a tendency to focus on myself and my problems.

The first few months of getting to know Tim and speaking with him on a regular basis I had never "looked" or really noticed his condition. I found him to be very intense and riveting when we would talk, and we just looked eye ball to eye ball, face to face.

It was quite a while before I became fully aware of the accident and came to know what he had been through. I never would have guessed. After he told me his neck had been broken, I noticed for the first time that he actually did need the cane.

In the months that followed I saw a man who did it all. He was the "manly provider" and then a "Mr. Mom." The amazing thing is that he did it very well. I asked him about it once, and he admitted at first it was a huge struggle. But he overcame it and absolutely cherished the time he could spend with his children. He's always adapting.

After a few years of knowing Tim I asked him to come to work for me in sales. My thoughts were: "If I can channel this attitude, this 'never-say-die attitude,' I will have a champion on my hands. I will not only be able to help him with an incredible income potential, but I will also help myself and my work load."

Tim had to undergo an interview with one of the experts in our field. He was the owner of our company, and, honestly, he did not want to hire Tim. After a pretty grueling question and answer session we brought Tim into the conference room. There the owner sat across from Tim. He slammed an unplugged desk phone down in front of him and said, "Okay, I'm your prospective customer. Sell me!" Tim kind of looked at him for a moment while the owner hollered again, "Sell me! Tell me why should I buy from you!" I'm off to the side dying at this point. I'm praying that God will give Tim the words - the guts - to go through with this!

Tim kind of smiled as he picked up the phone and started dialing. He pushed several buttons, taking his sweet time. Finally he spoke: "Hello. I'm calling for so and so, and I want to talk to him about... No! Wait!... Hello!? Hello!! Hello? Tim looked up right into the eyes of the owner and said, "Wow. Wrong number or not very interested I guess. Hmmm."

I was dead at this point, breathless and sick to

my stomach. I knew Tim had blown it. I felt so bad for him in that moment. A million thoughts raced through my head, and I couldn't think of anything to do. I think the owner of our company was stunned as well because he just sat there!

Then it happened. Tim looked the owner in the eye again and said, "You know Dean, that will happen. But the question is, 'What do you do about it?'"

Tim picked up the receiver and murmured, "You simply get another phone number and try again!" Tim then went through a 3-5 minute make-believe conversation with this imaginary prospect about why they should buy from us, how we will service their account, and how he will be sending the person follow up literature directly after the phone call. Flawless!

Another amazing aspect about Tim is his memory. It was like nothing I had seen. In my line of business - structured cabling components and hardware for communications systems - you don't go take a college course to learn it. You learn it in the field, and it takes quite a while. Within four months I had vendors calling on us in meetings and asking, "So where in this industry did Tim come from?" I would ask the question, "Tell me. How long do you think he's been in this business?" Their estimates ranged from five to ten years. When I explained his experience was in music they were flabbergasted.

Tim became my most trusted and hard working employee. I had a quota for all sales people to make at least 20 prospecting phone calls a day. It was quite a task to get most folks to follow through in making 20 calls. For Tim, it was nothing for him to turn in an average of 75 calls per day. He had no fear of rejection or objections.

I'll end this foreword with one last funny work story. After church on a Wednesday Tim had told me he was having some "funny pains" in his lower abdomen. I didn't think much of it, and neither did Tim.

The next day at work Tim mentioned again how strange it was that he hadn't felt anything near his waist since the accident, and he was actually feeling a little something. After thinking about this for a little bit, I told Tim he had to go to the doctor to get it checked out. He brushed me off at first, but I insisted. "Tim, you are numb! You regularly hit your leg on the metal desk while sitting down, and I have to tell you you're bleeding on your shoes!" If you can feel something, it could be something very bad like kidney problems."

Finally Tim gave in and went to see a doctor. He came to work the next day performing his daily balancing act of a coffee cup in one hand and cane in the other. I asked Tim, "Well, what did the doctor say?" As Tim put his coffee down he casually looked up at me and said, "Oh yeah, he said I'm passing several kidney stones." I asked him, "Right now? As we speak?" "Yeah," Tim said. "I can barely feel it, but at least I know what's going on."

I then told Tim that condition puts any man in bed and they are sick as dogs. They can't move! Tim then did a muscle man type pose in the office and said,

"Well, I guess I'm not just any man. That must be why the doctor was insisting I take some kind of pain medicine."

Over the last few years I have learned to laugh with Tim. I still learn many things from him as I watch him go through other struggles. I have never told Tim this, but it's the best summary or statement I can make about him in closing. But first let me quickly tell you this for reference sake. I was an athlete in school. I still work out a little bit. I'm six-foot, one and weigh 225 pounds. Tim Goonan, with his five-foot, nine-inch height and 150-pound body, is a true man - a fighter. He has shown more courage and more integrity while going through unthinkable trials than he would probably admit. God forbid that I may ever see half of the trials and tribulations Tim has seen. If I do, I hope I find that I am half the man he is.

Jeff Flint
Manufacturers Sales Representative
LAN* LINK Inc.

Introduction

The Fairytale Begins

Sometimes a challenge comes along in your life when you least expect it. When all is going well and everything is running smoothly, like an airplane on autopilot, something changes. The challenge may be large or small, but regardless of the size, when it strikes it can seem to overwhelm you with more than you can handle.

This book is entitled <u>Why Me? Why Not?, Making the Most Out of What You Have.</u> It is all about that question that burns within us when things in life do not go the way we would like them to go and we cry out: "Why Me?" The answer that I have found is: "Why Not?"

Circumstances occur in our lives that are not dependent upon whether you are a good or bad person. Things just happen to all of us that cannot be explained and are sometimes completely out of our control. Call it destiny or fate, but I believe that God created us all for a purpose. Now the trick is not to get confused with whether you think that what you are doing, at any given point in time, is important and big enough. Some of us are meant to do the little things well, and we were not destined to become a household name. We are just meant to "be" and to "do" the best we can with what we have.

This is why I have included in the title "Making the Most Out of What You Have". This is the key to being productive and finding those intangible things that you were created for - your moment in the spotlight. They will come and go sometimes without a lot of fanfare. These moments may change or evolve into something more than you first thought, or something different than what you had planned. Adapting to these changes is critical in obtaining balance and joy in what you are doing at any given moment in time. It is very important to remain open minded and flexible because once you have achieved a goal you need to be ready to do something that may be completely different from what you have done in the past.

My favorite word to live by in life has become "next." Something new is always around the corner! So with all of these things in mind, I am writing this book about a small piece of my life to share with my children and those who will follow me in this journey called life. I have no idea how many people will read what I write, and I am not vain enough to believe that this will ever make the best seller list at the bookstores. I pray that whoever reads this book will be touched by God through my story and encouraged to overcome whatever struggles they may have to face in this life. Believe in miracles, and give faith a chance. I wish you peace for your journey. Enjoy life's ride. It is all about what you make it!

My Background

I am a regular kind of a guy, born in a modest setting in Ohio to loving middle-class parents, Richard and Maryann, on October 6, 1957. My early life was filled with two things, baseball and music. I will always have a love for both of these activities and they are very much a part of the fabric of my life. I will not bore you with every detail of my childhood, but I just wanted you to know that it was pretty typical and common.

I have always been a dreamer. They have a name for it now, and it may even be considered a learning disability. But I became bored very easily with a task once I found that I could accomplish it. Born with a creative streak, art, sports, and music came naturally to me. I wish I would have worked harder to achieve higher goals in those areas. I became your classic underachiever, much to the dismay of my parents. I love the challenge and adventure of getting somewhere more than I actually enjoy arriving there. Quitting is not a word that I want in my vocabulary, and I have never been much for giving up. As a matter of fact, I have a hard time giving up.

I went into the military at the age of 17, and at the

time the military was not the most popular place to be. After Vietnam, many people didn't want to be associated with the military. I was proud that I served, and my motivation for serving was to get the GI Bill for a college education. I knew that my parents, having four other children, might not be able to send me to school. So I thought the best way to get a college education would be to have Uncle Sam pay my way in exchange for a pound of my flesh. It was a good experience, and I was able to grow up a little bit in the Navy. I was honorably discharged and returned home. I would like to thank my mother and father for their love and support that I have received all of my life. I was very fortunate to have such great parents.

After the military I started my college education at a local community college. My Uncle Dan told me to be a dentist because they make the big bucks, but I chose the most natural career path for me, which was music. I had several part-time summer jobs in college and enjoyed my first two years where I discovered that I could play the piano. My past music experience had always been as a vocalist, and I tried several instruments growing up. I tried the violin, trumpet and drums. Then I discovered the guitar. Teaching myself how to play by ear, I listened to records and learned how to play. I figured it out the hard way, like I did most lessons.

When I discovered the piano it was like finding a long lost friend, and I loved learning to play. I will always love my first piano teacher, Marilyn Montie.

She opened the doors to a beautiful world, and I will be eternally grateful for her life lessons as well as the piano lessons.

I blazed through the first few years of piano lessons in eight months, having a gift for playing that I never knew I had. It was an exciting period in my life, and I was a sponge as usual until the boredom set in. As always, I love the challenge until it is not a challenge anymore. After two years at a community college I ended up going to study at Bethel Collge with a great piano teacher named John Nordquist. But fate would intervene, and he had a heart attack at 40 years of age and died not long after that. It took the wind out of my sails. So in my third year of college I dropped out and found a job as an assistant manager at a Ponderosa Steak House.

I tried some rock bands and a Christian band, but nothing really happened with the career in music back then. I worked at a distribution center as well as several other small jobs trying to find my identity and a career path that I would find interesting. From there I married, and we soon started our family. I landed a great job at UPS, putting my life on a fast track. This is where I will begin the real story, and I hope that this short background has given you a small peek into my personality and where I come from.

Chapter One

My Fairytale

My life in November of 1989 was good. At the time I was happily married with two beautiful children, a nice home in the suburbs of Cleveland, Ohio, and a great job working for United Parcel Service. It was a life in the fast lane, on the fast track and moving up the ladder at UPS. Having just participated in a large corporate event with some of the upper level man-

Everything was under my control and working out, until fate would turn the page from the fairytale to the...

agement in attendance, I was on cloud nine. The event was a K.O.R.E. (Keeping Our Reputation for Excellence) seminar, and as a management candidate I had to give an oral presentation to several hundred people. Life was exciting, and I was dreaming of grabbing my piece of the "American Dream." I was finally on my way to UPS stock options, the fast track of management, more money than I could ever have dreamed of, and a professional career with a Fortune 500 company.

At the K.O.R.E. seminar I scored "extra points" because of my relationship with the guest keynote speaker, a field goal kicker. They had invited a professional football player to speak. I had no idea that Don Cockroft was going to be there. I knew him from church, and he was a close personal friend.

Don had played for the Cleveland Browns for several years, and when he saw me there in the crowd he ran over and gave me the traditional bear hug that somebody might give a long lost relative. We then spoke for several minutes about the kids and other personal things. It's funny how in a group of guys when you know a professional football player personally, they are suddenly in awe. It somehow validated my being there with the big boys. Tim was becoming somebody, at least in my small world from a limited point of view.

That October and November I was no longer a package car driver but a management candidate with the responsibility of training new drivers. Everything was under my control and working out, until fate would turn the page from the fairytale to the…

Chapter Two

When Tragedy Strikes

Tragedy.... According to Webster's Dictionary it means, 1 a : a medieval narrative poem or tale typically describing the downfall of a great man b : a serious drama typically describing a conflict between the protagonist and a superior force (as destiny) and having a sorrowful or disastrous conclusion that excites pity or terror : a disastrous event : CALAMITY b : MISFORTUNE 3 : tragic quality or element.

For me it kind of goes like this…

On November 18, 1989, I went to church on a Saturday morning to help put a new roof on a garage that we had built. It was always a good time hanging out with the guys and doing something that you do not do everyday. My wife picked me up around lunchtime with our children. We were on our way to the bank to cash the UPS check of the week and then home to eat. The sun was out and the skies were blue

…ahh the perfect life. As we were coming down our street, my daughter Samantha, who was a year old at the time, started to cry. Daddy was not going to let that happen. Taking my seatbelt off and reaching back to get her, I was holding her in my arms and comforting her when suddenly - Bang! I saw it coming, but I was helpless to do anything about it. I just held onto Samantha as tightly as I could. A car had run a stop sign five houses from where we lived. The impact came at the passenger side door and rolled our minivan. What only took seconds seemed like minutes to me and would effect the rest of our lives.

It's strange how life can suddenly seem as if it's moving in slow motion, almost like it's not really happening. As we rolled I was thrown between the two front seats, with part of my body still in the front seat and the other part coming to a rest face down on the backseat, where by the grace of God my daughter landed safely next to me.

I knew that I had broken my neck and that I was paralyzed. It felt like my body was attached to a generator that slowly ran out of gas, not just a quick on and off like a light switch, but a gradual slowing down to a stop. My body began to die. Yet at the very same moment my mind, spirit, and soul were never more alive.

A grace beyond measure and a joy came upon me, filling me with a quiet peace that surpasses all understanding. It was completely beyond reason, but it was a defining moment in my life. I knew that if I should take my last breath here on earth that I would be in Heaven.

So many random thoughts race through your mind in a situation such as this. Some thoughts were actually humorous, while others were very sad. I said goodbye to my wife and children telling them that it would be all right, and that I was ready to die. There was a strange quietness there that day, but my ears could hear so vividly all that was going on around me.

The quiet was soon replaced by the sounds of sirens and the voices of the paramedics as they arrived to do their best to save my life. My position in the van was very awkward, as I was wedged between the front and back seat, so it took a considerable amount of time to cut me out of the van. I heard the "jaws of life," saws and all of the other things that go along with an accident scene.

The quiet would soon be replaced by the sounds of sirens and the voices of the paramedics as they arrived to do their best to save my life.

I was so glad to hear that no one else was seriously injured. My family would be all right! My son T.J. and his cousin Richie were banged around, but God somehow kept everybody else free from any serious injuries. Thoughts raced through my mind like, "I am only 32 years old, and I thought I had more to do in life." Up to this point I had never broken a bone in my body, and now I'd broken a big one! Big changes. I had been listening to quadriplegic Joni Eareckson Tada on the radio in the mornings on my way to work. I suddenly knew what she had been through. I was so glad that I had heard her story before because it gave me hope that if I should live, I could still have a life. So many thoughts and barely able to breath, I heard the voices saying, "Hang in there Tim. Just hang in. Keep breathing." I took one breath, then another. Then I did what I have done all of my life for comfort. I sang in a small whispered voice, hearing the music from my heart and soul, "Amazing Grace how sweet the sound..." I got to take my first helicopter ride. Then the challenge began.

Chapter Three

Attitude, Attitude, Attitude

at·ti·tude: a position assumed for a specific purpose : a mental position with regard to a fact or state b : a feeling or emotion toward a fact or state...

Most of what I have to share and offer is based on this word "attitude." You either have a good and positive attitude, or a bad and negative attitude. If I can impart any words of wisdom to the reader at all, it will be to stay on the positive side of attitude, even in the most negative of circumstances.

With everything that I have experienced over the last 15 years, physically a terrible accident, emotionally a devastating divorce, financially a bankruptcy, and mentally more stress than I thought I would ever be capable of handling, it is safe to say that attitude played an important role in seeing me through all of the changes. This attitude combined with my faith, then mixed and shaken with my deep moral and spiritual convictions, have taught me valuable lessons

By permission. From Merriam-Webster's Collegiate® Dictionary, Eleventh Edition ©2004 by Merriam-Webster, Incorporated (Merriam-Webster.com).

about life. Here are four of the many lessons I've learned:

Lesson One: Humility

hu·mil·i·ty : the quality or state of being humble 1 : not proud or haughty : not arrogant or assertive 2 : reflecting, expressing, or offered in a spirit of deference or submission...

The swishing of the helicopter blades was amazing to my ears and sounded like a rhythmic symphony. Here was my first chance at a helicopter ride, and I couldn't see out the window. Bummer! It was still kind of exciting and fun to me, as I have always been a big kid at heart. Even to this day at 42 years of age, I am still intimately in touch with my inner child, as many who know me would probably agree to as a fact.

As we touched down, the emergency team went into action. The hustle and bustle of the nurses, as they worked to make me as stable and as comfortable as possible, would soon be replaced with a strange loneliness as I lay on a cart with a thin white sheet covering me. In emergency situations like this, you are immediately humbled as they cut all of the clothing off of your body. I had never had so many people look at my naked body in such a short span. I felt completely at the will of those around me. I was poked and prodded, and much to my amazement I couldn't feel a thing.

Being paralyzed at least has one advantage: you feel no pain. When you are completely paralyzed there is no escape. I couldn't get up or move a muscle, and by that time my neck and head were completely immobilized. So I just laid there in silence, waiting and wondering what would be next.

Listening becomes very interesting. My ears were somehow affected, and I had an incredible ability to hear in those moments. Perhaps I had never listened quite as hard before, but they say your body will sometimes compensate for a disability by overcompensating in other areas. I felt like Superman as I listened to conversations that I probably wasn't supposed to hear. I knew from the conversations that I had ruptured the vertebrae in my neck at the C6 and C7 level. I then learned there was a chance that if they had to go through the front of my neck to repair the damage that I could die during the procedure. All I could do was listen and pray. Humbled at last. The circumstances were far beyond my control now, and in the hands of God and these wonderful people that I did not know. I've always had an independent spirit, and now, completely dependent on others to take care of me and all of my needs, I had an attitude of humility.

Lesson Two: Gratitude

grat·i·tude 1 : the state of being grateful : THANKFUL-
NESS...

Have you ever been really grateful about something small? I have. Back in 1989, I began to learn
about gratitude for what we all take for granted in our
everyday lives. Take tying your shoe as an example.
Most people have the ability to pick up a shoe and
get it onto their foot, bend over and grasp the shoe-
laces in both hands. Most people can manipulate the
strings to form a knot. In 1989 I could no longer accomplish this simple task. How about breathing on
your own? It doesn't seem all that complicated until
you lose the ability to do it. We all face these types of
struggles, but to a lesser degree than what being paralyzed will do to you. I became so thankful for the little
things in life, and I made a conscious decision to do
the best I could with whatever ability I had left.

The point that I am trying to make is crucial for
you in your everyday life. If you can learn to appreciate what you have and not dwell on what you don't
have, then you will gain an ability to focus on what
you can do instead of what you cannot do. This attitude of thanksgiving will open up to you a world of
looking at the glass as half full instead of half empty,

By permission. From Merriam-Webster's Collegiate® Dictionary,
Eleventh Edition ©2004 by Merriam-Webster, Incorporated
(Merriam-Webster.com).

giving you an ability to excel.

The second part of being grateful is to express gratitude to the people that you are dependent on, whether you realize it or not. We do not call the gas company or the electric company to thank all of the individual people that work at those companies. Yet they ensure, by their diligent work, that we have electricity for the heater, coffee on cold mornings, and the lights we see at night.

Have you ever had an itchy nose or back? In the hospital there were times when I prayed and waited for somebody, anybody, to walk into my room to scratch the itch. My nose would itch and itch, with no way for me to relieve the discomfort. It seems like such a small thing, but we all have needs that others meet, both large and small. But do we make a practice out of being grateful for their efforts? Or do we take them for granted as just people, "doing their jobs?"

When we learn to be grateful for what others are doing on our behalf, we can become better managers or employees. We can become better husbands, wives, parents, friends and people when we possess a thankful spirit. When I lost my physical ability to do the little things I gained a deeper appreciation for those around me who took such good care of me and met my needs. Please let the people that are a part of your everyday life hear the words "thank you."

Lesson Three: Perseverance

per·se·ver·ance STEADFASTNESS : to persist in a state, enterprise, or undertaking in spite of counterinfluences, opposition, or discouragement...

Have you ever waited on something or someone for any length of time? Did you look at the clock and wonder whether you were lost in the shuffle? As your patience starts to dwindle, you start weighing whether it is worth the time to wait or not.

There was a time that I recall one such wait. In the hospital I had to undergo several routine x-rays. Afterwards, I was taken out and left in the hallway where I was to wait for somebody to take me back to the room. They placed me under the worst piece of artwork that I had ever seen in my life, but that picture was all I had to look at for the next several hours. You see, I had been lost in the shuffle. There was nobody there to rescue me and to take me back to my room. I waited with much patience and learned that at times things are not in your control.

They eventually found me, and I made it back to the room, but I will never forget how that picture grew on me as I began to look for the good in that bad art. I found some qualities that I would never have seen with my initial glance because I would not have stud-

By permission. From Merriam-Webster's Collegiate® Dictionary, Eleventh Edition ©2004 by Merriam-Webster, Incorporated (Merriam-Webster.com).

ied it long enough to discover what the artist was trying to convey. Always look for the good in the bad.

This could be my longest chapter by far if I were to relay all of the experiences I've had that involve perseverance. We all have to persevere from the cradle to the grave. As a parent I remember watching my children learn to walk. They would try to stand and plop right back down as gravity, and their sense of equilibrium not being fully developed, would pull them down to the floor. Then I watched their first steps and failures. I noticed their persistence.

At 32 years of age, I had to begin learning to walk all over again. Physical therapy is truly an amazing thing. They bend you and move you when you cannot move yourself, in directions that you never thought imaginable. There were times when they moved my legs to places that I could not have moved them before the accident. The first time I tried to stand up again, after being told that I never would stand or walk again, I became dizzy and lightheaded. Struggling and sweating to make my muscles respond to the mental commands to walk, I had forgotten how tall I was from sitting in a wheelchair for so long. In the wheelchair everyone around you looks very tall. Standing up again, my physical therapist Louise suddenly looked her 5 feet tall instead of the 6 feet tall that I imagined, and I realized that I was actually around 5-feet,10-inches and not the 4 feet tall I had become in the wheelchair. It's so easy to lose your perspective when things change who you are.

Learning to stand and walk again took every ounce of energy and intestinal fortitude that I could muster. I would slowly drag myself down the parallel bars while holding my weight up with my arms. Inch by inch, foot by foot, and eventually through perseverance I learned to walk in a different new way. I used what I had, not what was gone. It would have been easier to quit, because I had become accustomed to the wheelchair by this point, and I had learned to get around pretty well in it.

Fortunately perseverance requires you to take one more step if you can, so I felt compelled to press forward, never quitting or losing hope of the possibilities that lay ahead… unafraid to fail.

One of my father's favorite stories to tell (you can always tell when a parent gets that excitement in their voice and twinkle in the eye) was the story from an amusement park when I was a child. They had a contest where you tied the balloon around your foot, and then 30 or 40 kids ran around this big circle trying to step on the other guys balloon. Well it boiled down to me against two other boys that were obviously good friends. I think they must have chased me for fifteen minutes before the people running the contest called it off and made all three of us winners. If you hang in there long enough, then something good is bound to happen, even if winning means sharing the prize.

My favorite book on perseverance comes from the Bible. Job is one of many men I admire in the Old Testament. As I read Job I began to feel like I didn't

34

have it so bad after all. Job lost everything: his family, his possessions and his health. If you look beyond yourself at the world around you, then you will see there's always somebody in a worse situation than you. If you see them rise above it all and live, then let it be an inspiration to you as you walk through the valley of circumstance with an attitude of perseverance. I have now learned the attitude of perseverance.

Lesson Four: Adaptability

adapt·abil·i·ty : to make fit (as for a specific or new use or situation) often by modification to become adapted synonyms ADAPT, ADJUST, ACCOMMODATE, CONFORM, RECONCILE...

Making changes at even the smallest level can throw a family or a person into a panic. Things so simple as having to change your hairstyle or carpet can become monumental decisions. When those decisions affect others, they can become very complicated and difficult to make. The longer you live, though, you'll learn that the one thing besides taxes and death that you can count on will be change.

Knowing this ahead of time, you may want a few tips to prepare for change. Here's the tip: don't bother making too many plans because usually the change is either gradual and you can't see it, or it pounces on you like a hungry lion. Instead, learn to change the way you think about changes. I like to look at the problem of making changes from the perspective of adventure. If we view life as a journey and mentally accept change as an opportunity to experience something new and exciting, then we can adapt to the circumstances and environment around us. The constant in the equation of life should be what we really are on the inside, our character and the spirit and soul that can drive our distinctive personalities.

Having made so many changes in the last 15 years, I can't keep up with them all. Learning to adapt with what you have is the key to making the most out of what you have. As I wheeled around in the hospital, they used to tell me not to carry objects with my teeth because it could hurt them. This makes perfect sense until you need to carry an object and your hands are busy providing the muscle to wheel there. Adapting may at times mean sacrifice and compromise.

One of my most prized processions is a work of art that I did while in the hospital over three months. I had to find a way to adapt in occupational therapy to accomplish a goal. I started by using my teeth (I know. Shame on me.) to get a hard stick into a device called a quad cuff. When you have no grip, the quad cuff gives a paralyzed person the ability to do tasks like brushing your teeth. In this case it helped me in making an image in tin. I did "The Last Supper" from an imprint. I had to find a way to press down hard enough to make the imprint come through. This took weeks to accomplish, using my chin, shoulders, mouth, hands and mind to get the job done. I had to adapt to the environment and my circumstances.

One of the most discouraging times that I have ever faced was coming home from the hospital for a few hours at Christmas. It was as if I could hear my piano calling out to me, "Play me. You remember how."

In my mind I could still play. They wheeled me over to the piano, and I could barely press a key down with my thumb. My fingers did not work, and to this day they still do not function properly. Tears fell as my heart broke, facing the reality that I would never again play like I had before the accident.

It was as if I could hear my piano calling out to me, "Play me. You remember how."

Now self-pity is not a great virtue of mine, but at times anger can become a useful tool when controlled. I chose to get angry and not give up. Thinking it would be good therapy for my hands, I decided that I would learn to play somehow with what I had left. A computer would help me get the music out of my head. I thought to myself, "I can hear the music, and I know the notes. I have my thumbs. Someday I will make the music." Over the course of the last 11 years I have found a way to adapt and use the fingers that work, the way they work, to play the guitar and piano again. I may never play Carnegie Hall, but I have become a successful songwriter to a minor degree in Nashville. Some of my songs have been recorded, and I'm not done yet. I plan on writing songs that you will someday hear on the radio and television. Remember the perseverance lesson? Combine that lesson with an ability to adapt and change, and then…Think Big or Stay Home.

Chapter Four

Think Big...or Stay Home

I have a friend who shared with me something that her grandmother told her. It is an approach to life that I like when combined with the idea of being content in what you have. It's called, "Think Big or Stay Home." When we dream we ought to dream of the best. It's kind of like those monster.com commercials during the Super Bowl, where the little children are saying what they want to be when they grow up. Things like, "I want to be stuck in middle management," or "I want to have a low-paying job and never accomplishing much of anything in life."

We can get comfortable to the point of not thinking big enough. I started a business as a search and recruitment specialist, affectionately known to some as a headhunter. Thinking big is what I choose to do, and over the course of the first year I have seen some successes. Taking the risk of starting this was difficult, but I had nothing else going at the time, and now

I am thinking big and staying home as I work out of my house. Still, I have the desire to grow my business, or another business in music, over the next five years, so that I may allow others an opportunity to succeed.

My theory is that when you take the focus off of yourself and try to help others become more successful, this is where the "big" comes into play. Our world is so big, but we seldom see those around us that we can help. Usually in this process of helping others we end up benefiting ourselves financially and personally. You can never have too many friends and acquaintances. Today our world is driven by the ability to network effectively and to keep pace with the constant changes in technology. Business is conducted at blazing speeds with the Internet, but the underlying current remains the same. Business is still forged by relationships and the ability to communicate when you represent yourself to others.

Business is still a contact sport. At times it can still be who you know and whether you have the kind of relationship with the client that makes them comfortable. In those "all things being equal" situations between you and a competitor, will they choose your services or products because of you? Probably. So think big and walk with some confidence that you are worth choosing… or stay home.

Chapter Five
F.A.I.L.U.R.E.

fail·ure 1 a : omission of occurrence or performance; specifically : a failing to perform a duty or expected action b : a state of inability to perform a normal function...

Examine my definition of failure:

F is for Future,
A is for Achiever,
I is for In,
L is for Life, F.A.I.L.
U is for YOU,
R is for ARE, and last but not least
E is for Exceptional and Experienced !!!

Future Achievers In Life Club - You Are Exceptional and Experienced !

Life is about learning, and the most valuable lessons gained are often taught to us through experience. There will always be some lessons that cannot be acquired through books. You can get the knowledge of what to do, but until you experience the lesson you will never know for sure that you can accomplish the task. As a corporate search and recruitment specialist, I am very aware that companies will base the decision to use my services on whether it is worth paying a fee for my candidate's unique experience combined with any required skills. If the candidate can bring enough experience to the bargaining table it can justify the expense.

There is an old tried and true method for taking risks, and it is called the trial and error method. At times in the learning process it is the only way to gain the experience necessary to grow. When we take a risk we will at times become acquainted, in an intimate and uncomfortable way, with failure. Look at it realistically. You cannot be the best at everything, but you can try your best in everything you do. In this process of trying we learn to develop our natural resources to accomplish what we can do. We learn to accept our limitations and move on toward what we can achieve. We also learn to work around our limitations or find others to network with who possess an ability to accomplish what we cannot.

A marathon is a grueling 26.2 mile test of a person's ability to endure pain and the human spirit and mind's willingness to rise above the "wall." The wall is a point in the race where you believe that you cannot take another step. Then, you take one more step despite what your mind believes you can endure and find yourself in a zone that enables you to continue. No longer able to run in a marathon, I learned to push in a marathon while strapped into a wheelchair. Did I cross the finish line? Yes! Although my body failed to run, I overcame a disability to accomplish a goal. I found a new way to compete, and then I networked with others who had an ability to make a racing wheelchair to push my way to the finish line.

We are all exceptional, but the only way that you will ever find what you can accomplish is to take the risk of failing. Every time you fail, remember that it was just one more step to becoming all that you can be. So welcome to the Future Achievers In Life club. You Are Exceptional and Experienced ! Now use it in a positive way to be all that you were meant to be.

Another acronym for failure is:

F is for Fear
A is for Acknowledge
I is for Improvise
L is for Learn
U is for Use
R is for Risk
E is for Evaluate

I believe that FEAR is one of the greatest enemies we face. We allow fear to paralyze our abilities to be creative, to move forward and to live life to the fullest. To overcome this fear, my first step was to ACKNOWLEDGE the fear and then put it where it belongs. Most fear was meant to be a caution light. True danger gets the red light and has little to do with fear and more to do with common sense. We use fire to cook food with, but we know the "red light" when working with fire. Common sense tells us not to stick our hand into the flame. If the kitchen starts on fire, then the fear we feel must be the caution light that senses the apparent danger prompting us to move to a safe place. If you stand still and allow fear to paralyze you in that situation you may lose your life. We need to assess the danger or risk and then move somewhere!

Things that do not move are usually dead or dying. We can look around at creation for this lesson. Water that moves has life, but water that is still becomes stagnant and evaporates until nothing is left. At times in life we move forward, sometimes to the side, and at other times we may need to take that step backward to look at what we are trying to accomplish from a different point of view. It is with this "new point of view" where we can learn to IMPROVISE. I have seen through music and acting how this works. Often, the only person who knows that you have forgotten a line, made a mistake, or played a different note will be you. If you continue to play and make the best of the experience, most of the audience may never realize the error and still appreciate the performance. When you stop, everyone can see the mistake. The idea here is to accomplish the goal first as you complete the task, then assess how you can improve the process.

We often LEARN much more by living in the lab

called life. Once you gain knowledge from experience, it's time to USE what you have learned, but this requires RISK. At some point you must learn to EVALUATE what you have learned through failure. Then, take a proper risk to try again. When you learn how to take an acceptable risk, you will grow and become all that you can be. If you can change how you look at failure and develop an attitude that leaves fear behind, then you will find a freedom to pursue your dreams and goals.

Chapter Six
Finding Your Balance

bal·ance : an instrument for weighing: a means of judging or deciding a counterbalancing weight, force, or influence: equality between the totals of the two sides of an account: physical equilibrium: the ability to retain one's balance: mental and emotional steadiness: with all things considered.

One line from a song that I have enjoyed listening to states, "there will be highs and lows..." Having been up to the mountaintop and way down in the valley below, I will admit that balance can be an elusive word that is more easily said than done. Emotions do not take balance well. Still, balance must be achieved to accomplish the goals that we set for ourselves. Over the years I have seen a great deal of literature on proper goal setting and the value of setting attainable goals mixed with a goal that seems impossible to achieve. But the impossible goal is my favorite, because it is the goal that stirs hope in the heart and can push you to the limit of your abilities and endurance. It is this goal, the one that involves risk and a real potential for failure, where balance is acquired through experience. This daring to dream, as I like to call it, creates an environment where conflict is possible. However, the resolution through balance teaches the dreamer to accept losses.

Accepting loss and the inability to accomplish the goal as you might have envisioned may lead to thinking of other ways to achieve the goal. Hopefully this process will produce the perseverance to try again, knowing what you experience and learn along the way will be far greater in the development of your character than the attainment of the goal. Remember, there are no rules to follow when you dream and set a goal. You can refine, change, and adapt your goals at any time without penalty. (A little soccer humor. Goals? Penalty?)

While moving through the many phases of physical therapy I had to find proper balance in more ways than one. Learning to walk again meant finding balance the best way that I could with what I had available physically. My cane is an example of proper balance. Without it I am doomed to fall at some point, somewhere. With it I achieve a higher sense of balance. This works until I close my eyes. I will compare this in a figurative way to our emotional responses at times, because with my eyes closed I have no sense of balance at all. The only way to achieve my proper balance is to recognize when I will have my eyes closed.

At those times I make sure I am sitting or lying down so as to remain balanced in a safe way. The cane is my reality in a figurative sense, and it's just a tool to help me attain a higher sense of balance. For you, the cane or tool may be something like music or working out at the gym. It is something that is not a part of us, but outside of who we are.

We all need a balance or a crutch, so to speak, at times to counter emotional and physical highs and lows. The highs during the recovery period in my life were very high and the lows were very low. I had to grieve over the loss of my physical abilities and the life that I had set in motion with all of my goals and dreams. I managed to learn to balance these two very different emotions. The high being the success in learning to walk again in a different way, contrasted with the failure of not being able to ever run again as a low. Both were goals, one achievable and one not achievable, but both served a purpose in helping me to recognize a balance that I would need to sustain me through the emotions that accompany loss.

Everybody gets the blues, and we all fear what we do not know. Just try to remember that you are not alone with these feelings, and that they are extremely common.

Some other outside influences that can effect your balance in life during a crisis are the fear (here's that word again) of the unknown and depression. If you have ever had either of these emotions then you are completely human. Everybody gets the blues, and we all fear what we do not know. Just try to remember that you are not alone with these feelings, and that they are extremely common. Do not be afraid to find people you respect and trust. If things get really bad, then swallow your pride and get some professional help from a counselor or therapist.

I had never understood depression, and I had always been optimistic about most situations until I went through the accident and a divorce. I thought I could handle most of my problems on my own, and I would internalize them and not seek help from those around me. The problem with that approach is that in order to attain a better balance we need to get some input from external sources. I believe that after having gone through a severe depression following my divorce, I learned something new about proper balance that others have known for centuries. We can lose all objectivity if the only person we rely on for counsel is ourselves. It has been the downfall of kings and empires!

To achieve a proper balance, face fear head on for what it is: a yellow flashing sign saying "be careful and think." Don't let it be a stop sign that can paralyze your ability to take proper risks. Then, take counsel from others to avoid the consequences of internalizing to the point of depression. Depression is like being in a coma. A coma is your body's natural defense to protect you for a short period of time while your body heals. Depression slows you down to grieve and heal your mind and soul, but you cannot stay there. Seek help. Eventually you must leave the low to find the balance. Remember that there will be highs and lows. Try to spend most of your time in a balanced state between the two.

Chapter Seven

Tapping Into the Power Source

This chapter is one that I am compelled to share with you. My intention is not to insult anyone with my religious beliefs and faith. I am not dogmatic on one religious denomination being the only correct faith. I have participated in many different denominations at various times in my journey, and they all have something that I do agree with and something that I do not agree with. My power to press forward comes from God.

I am a Christian and I currently attend First Baptist Church in Hendersonville, Tennessee. I have shared my story with many people and churches of various denominations in the past. Where God tells me to worship is where I will worship. I will go and speak to anyone that will invite me in. I do not intend to convert anyone to the way I worship or my faith. That is God's job, but I intend on telling everybody who might ask where I have found my joy and power. It is in the same power God used to raise Jesus from the dead.

I'll close with one last hospital story. When I was going through physical therapy, I recall a unique experience with electrical stimulation. This is the process where they strategically place electrodes on places where the nerves are close to the surface. Then they shoot electricity through the electrodes to make your muscles move.

My therapist attached each electrode to my legs at all of the key areas, and then she turned on the power switch. What she didn't know was that the control was on the highest setting that the unit would allow. In an instant I found my legs and feet up to my ears and over my head. In a calm voice I told her that I thought it might be up a little too high because my legs had never been that flexible. We laughed about it, and she turned it off and apologized too many times. It didn't hurt, but it's an illustration to show you that if you tap into the biggest power source available, then you can do the impossible. I could never have gotten my legs that far had I not been paralyzed. I could never have made it this far in my journey without God's power in my life.

I received a miracle from God that allows me to walk, even though it is with a cane. I know that it is a miracle, and the doctors who provided care for me at the hospital know that they have seen a miracle. Too much time had gone by, with no return of motion after the initial accident, for my body to have progressed to the point of me being able to walk again. I know this. Some will believe and some will not. Like all of the miracles that God has done throughout time, the awesomeness seems to fade. The miracles Jesus did have faded into history, and some people have tried to explain them in a logical and rational way.

There is no logical way to accept the impossible, except to believe in faith. If you are curious as to what faith means and we meet at some time in the future, ask me what FAITH stands for because I would love to share with you what I have learned. While I'm alive I will be a living witness and testimony to the real Power Source - the source of my strength in weakness. I pray that you will find this same peace with God the Father that I have found through Jesus, and with the ultimate power source, through His Holy Spirit. I wish you peace for you journey with faith, hope and love… the greatest of these gifts being love.

Look for the forthcoming Bible study
based on *Why Me? Why Not? Making
the Most Out of What You Have* and
other titles from

Little Giants
Publishing, Inc.

If you enjoyed this book or have com-
ments, please contact the publisher at
www.littlegiants.net